ארבעתאל

Of the
MAGICK
of the
Ancients,

The greatest Study of Wisdom.

"In all things, ask counsel of the Lord; and do not you think, speak, or do anything, wherein God is not your counsellor."

Proverbs II

"He that walketh fraudulently, revealeth secrets: but he that is of a faithful spirit, concealeth the matter."

ARBATEL of MAGICK:

OR,

The spiritual Wisdom of the Ancients,
as well Wise-men of the people of God,
as MAGI of the Gentiles: for the illustration of
the glory of God, and his
love to Mankind.

Now first of all produced out of darkness into the light, against all caco-Magicians, and contemners of the gifts of God; for the profit and delegation of all those, who do truely and piously love the creatures of God, and do use them with thanksgiving, to the honour of God, and profit of themselves and their neighbours.

Containing nine Tomes and Seven Septenaries of
APHORISMS.

The first is called Isagoge, or, A Book of the Institutions of Magick: or, *ἡ παιδματικῆς* which in fourty and nine Aphorisms comprehends the most general Precepts of the whole Art.

The second is Microcosmical Magick, what *Microcosmus* has effected Magically, by his Spirit and Genius effected to him from his Nativity, that is, spiritual wisdom: and how the same is effected.

The third is Olympic Magick, in what manner a man may do and suffer by the spirits of Olympus,

The fourth is Hesiodiacal, and Homerical Magick, which teaches the operations by the Spirits called Cacodæmons as it were not adversaries to mankind.

The fifth is Roman or Sibylline Magick, which acts and operates with Tutelar Spirits and Lords, to whom the whole Orb of the earth is distributed. This is *valde insignis Magia*. To this also is the doctrine of the Druids referred.

The sixth is Pythagorical Magick, which only acts with Spirits to whom is given the doctrine of Arts, as Physic, Medicines, Mathematics, Alchemy, and such kind of Arts.

The seventh is the Magick of Apollonius, and the like, and agrees with the Roman and Microcosmical Magick: only it has this thing peculiar, that it has power over the hostile spirits of mankind.

The eighth is Hermetical, that is, Ægyptiacal Magick; and differs not much from Divine Magick.

The ninth is that wisdom which depends solely upon the Word of God; and this is called Prophetical Magick.

The First Tome of the Book of Arbatel of Magick, Called ISAGOGE.

IN the Name of the Creator of all things both visible and invisible, who reveals his Mysteries out of his Treasures to them that call upon him; and fatherly and mercifully bestowes those his Secrets upon us without measure. May he grant unto us, through his only-begotten Son Jesus Christ our Lord, his ministring spirits, the revealers of is secrets, that we may write this Book of Arbatel concerning the greatest Secrets which are lawful for man to know, and to use them without offence unto God. Amen.

The first Septenary of Aphorisms.

The first Aphorism,

Whosoever would know Secrets, let him know how to keep secret things secretly; and to reveal those things that are to be revealed, and to seal those things which are to be sealed: and not to give holy things to dogs, nor cast pearls before swine. Observe this Law and the eyes of your Understanding shall be opened, to understand secret things; and you shall have whatsoever your mind desires to be divinely revealed unto you. You shall have also the Angels and Spirits of God prompt and ready in their nature to minister unto you, as much as any human mind can desire.

Aphor. 2.

In all things, call upon the Name of the Lord: and without prayer unto God through his only-begotten Son, do not you undertake to do or think any thing. And use the Spirits given and attributed unto you, as Ministers, without rashness and presumption, as the messengers of God; having a due reverence towards the Lord of Spirits. And the remainder of your life do you accomplish, demeaning your self peaceably, to the honour of God, and the profit of your self and your neighbour.

Aphor. 3.

Live to your self, and the Muses: avoid the friendship of the Multitude: be you covetous of time, beneficial to all men. Use your Gifts, be vigilant in your Calling; and let the Word of God never depart from your mouth.

Aphor. 4.

Be obedient to good Admonitions: avoid all procrastination: accustom your self to Constancy and Gravity, both in your words and deeds. Resist the temptations of the Tempter, by the Word of God. Flee from earthly things; seek after heavenly things. Put no confidence in your own wisdom; but look unto God in all things, according to that sentence of the Scripture: when we know not what we shall do, unto you O God do we lift up our eyes, and from you we expect our help. For where all human refuges do forsake us, there will the help of God shine forth, according to the saying of Philo.

Aphor. 5.

You shall love the Lord your God with all your heart; and with all your strength, and your neighbour as your self: And the Lord will keep you as the apple of his eye, and will deliver you from all evil, and will replenish you with all good; and nothing shall your soul desire, but you shall be fully endued therewith, so that it be contingent to the salvation of your soul and body.

Aphor. 6.

Whatsoever you have learned, frequendy repeat, and fix the same in your mind: and learn much,but not many things, because a human undemanding cannot be alike capable in all things, unless it be such a one that is divinely regenerated; unto him nothing is so difficult or manifold, which he may not be able equally to attain to.

Aphor. 7.

Call upon me in the day of trouble, and I will hear you and you shall glorify me, says the Lord. For all Ignorance is tribulation of the mind; therefore call upon the Lord in your

Ignorance, and he will hear you. And remember that you give honour unto God, and say with the Psalmist, *Not unto us, Lord, not unto us, but unto your Name give the glory.*

The second Septenary of Aphorisms.

The eighth Aphorism,

Even as the Scripture testifies, that God appoints names to things or persons, and also with them has distributed certain powers and offices out of his treasures: so the Characters and Names of Stars have not any power by reason of their figure or pronunciation, but by reason of the virtue or office which God has ordained by nature either to such a Name or Character. For there is no power either in heaven or in earth, or hell, which does not descend from God; and without his permission, they can neither give or draw forth into any action, any thing they have.

Aphor. 9.

That is the chiefest wisdom, which is from God; and next, that which is in spiritual creatures; afterwards, in corporal creatures; fourthly, in Nature and natural things. The Spirits that are apostate, and reserved to the last judgement, do follow these, after a long interval. Sixthly, the ministers of punishments in hell,and the obedient unto God. Seventhly, the Pigmies do not possess the lowest place, and they who inhabit in elements, and elementary things. It is convenient therefore to know and discern all differences of the wisdom of the Creator and the Creatures, that it may be certainly manifest unto us, what we ought to assume to our use of every thing, and that we may know in truth how and in what manner that may be done. For truely every creature is ordained for some profitable end to human nature, and for the service thereof; as the holy Scriptures, Reason, and Experience, do testify.

Aphor. 10.

God the Father Almighty, Creator of heaven and earth, and of all things visible and invisible, in the holy Scriptures proposes himself to have an eye over us; and as a tender father which loves his children, he teaches us what is profitable, and what not; what we are to avoid, and what we are to embrace: then he allures us to obedience with great promises of corporal and eternal benefits, and deters us (with threatening of punishments) from those things which are not profitable for us. Turn over therefore with your hand, both night and day, those holy Writings, that you may be happy in things present, and blessed to all eternity. Do this, and you shall live, which the holy Books have taught you.

Aphor. 11.

A number of four is Pythagorical, and the first: Quadrate; therefore here let us place the foundation of all wisdom, after the wisdom of God revealed in the holy Scriptures, and to the Considerations proposed in Nature. Appoint therefore to him who solely depends upon God, the wisdom of every creature to serve and obey him, *nolens volens*, willing or unwilling. And in this, the Omnipotency of God shines forth. It consists therefore in this, that we will discern the creatures which serve us, from those that are unwilling; and that we may learn how to accommodate the wisdom and offices of every creature unto our selves. This Art is not delivered, but divinely. Unto whom God will, he reveals his secrets; but to whom he will not bestow any thing out of his treasuries, that person shall attain to nothing without the will of God. Therefore we ought truely to desire *τλὼ πνδμμανκλὼ ὅπσηρλὼ* from God alone, which will mercifully impart these things unto us. For he who has given us his Son, and commanded us to pray for his holy Spirit, How much more will he subject unto us the whole creature, and things visible and invisible? *Whatsoever you ask you shall receive.* Beware that you do not abuse the gifts of God, and all things shall work together unto you for your salvation. And before all things, be watchful in this, That your names be written in heaven: this is more light, That the spirits be obedient unto you, as Christ admonishes.

Aphor. 12.

In the Acts of the Apostles, the Spirit says unto Peter after the Vision, Go Down and doubt not but, have sent them, when he was sent for from Cornelius the Centurion. After this manner, in vocal words, are all disciplines delivered, by the holy Angels of God, as it appears one of the Monuments of the Ægyptians. And these things afterwards were vitiated and corrupted with human opinions; and by the instigation of evil spirits, who sow tares amongst the children of disobedience, as it is manifest out of St. Paul, and Hermes

Trismegistus. There is no other manner of restoring these Arts, then by the doctrine of the holy Spirits of God; because true faith comes by hearing. But because you may be certain of the truth, and may not doubt whether the spirits that speak with you, do declare things true or false, let it only depend upon your faith in God; that you may say with Paul, I know on whom I trust. If no sparrow can fall to the ground without, the will of the Father which is in heaven, How much more will not God suffer you to be deceived, O you of little faith, if you depend wholly upon God, and adhere only to him?

Aphor. 13.

The Lord lives; and all things which live, do live in him. And he is truely יהוה who has given unto all things, that they be that which they are: and by his word alone, through his Son, has produced all things out of nothing, which are in being. He calls all the stars, and all the host of heaven by their names. He therefore knows the true strength and nature of things, the order and policy of every creature visible and invisible, to whom God has revealed the names of his creatures. It remains also, that he receive power from God, to extract the venues in nature, and hidden secrets of the creature; and to produce their power into action, out of darkness into light. Your scope therefore ought to be, that you have the names of the Spirits, that is, their powers and offices, and how they are subjected and appointed by God to minister unto you; even as Raphael was sent to Tobias, that he should heal his father, and deliver his son from dangers, and bring him to a wife. So Michael the fortitude of God governs the people of God: Gabriel, the messenger of God, was sent to Daniel, Mary, and Zachary the father of John Baptist. And he shall be given to you that desire him, who will teach you whatsoever your soul shall desire, in the nature of things. His ministry you shall use with trembling and fear of your Creator, Redeemer, and Sanctifier, that is to say, the Father,Son, and holy Ghost: and do not you let slip any occasion of learning, and be vigilant in your calling, and you shall want nothing that is necessary for you.

Aphor. 14.

Your soul lives forever, through him that has created you: call therefore upon the Lord your God, and him only shall you serve. This you shall do, if you will perform that end for which you are ordained of God, and what you owe to God and to your neighbour. God requires of you a mind, that you should honour his Son, and keep the words of his Son in your heart: if you honour him, you have done the will of your Father which is in heaven. To your neighbour you owe offices of humanity, and that you draw all men that come to you, to honour the Son. This is the Law and the Prophets. In temporal things, you ought to call upon God as a father, that he would give unto you all necessities of this life: and you ought to help your neighbour with the gifts which God bestows upon you, whether they be spiritual or corporal.

Therefore you shall pray thus:

O Lord of heaven and earth, Creator and Maker of all things visible and invisible, I, though unworthy, by your assistance call upon you, through your only-begotten Son Jesus Christ our Lord, that you will give unto me your holy Spirit, to direct me in your truth unto all good. Amen. Because I earnestly desire perfectly to know the Arts of this life, and such things as are necessary for us, which are so over-whelmed in darkness, and polluted with infinite human opinions, that I of my own power can attain to no knowledge in them, unless you teach it me: Grant me therefor one of your spirits, who may teach me those things which you would have me to know and learn, to your praise and glory, and the profit of our neighbour. Give me also an apt and teachable heart, that I may easily understand those things which you shall teach me, and may hide them in my understanding, that I may bring them forth as out of your inexhaustible treasures, to all necessary uses. And give me grace, that I may use such your gifts humbly, with fear and trembling, through our Lord Jesus Christ, with your holy Spirit. Amen.

The fifteenth Aphorism,

They are called Olympic spirits, which do inhabit in the firmament, and in the stars of the firmament: and the office of these spirits is to declare Destinies, and to administer fatal Charms, so far forth as God pleases to permit them: for nothing, neither evil spirit nor evil Destiny, shall be able to hurt him who has the most High for his refuge. If therefore any of the Olympic spirits shall reach or declare that which his star to which he is appointed portends, nevertheless he can bring forth nothing into action, unless he be permitted by the Divine power. It is God alone who gives them power to effect it, Unto God the maker of all things, are obedient all things celestial, sublunary, and infernal. Therefore rest in this: Let God be your guide in all things which you undertake and all things shall attain to a happy and desired end; even as the history of the whole world testifies, and daily experience shows. There is peace to the godly: there is no peace to the wicked, says the Lord.

Aphor. 16.

There are seven different governments of the Spirits of Olympus, by whom God has appointed the whole frame and universe of this world to be governed: and their visible stars are ARATRON, BETHOR, PHALEG, OCH, HAGITH, OPHIEL, PHUL, after the Olympic speech. Every one of these has under him a mighty Militia in the firmament.

Aratron rules visible Provinces XLIX.

Bethor, XXXII.

Phaleg, XXXV

Och, XXVIII.

Hagith, XXI.

Ophiel, XIIII.

Phul, VII.

So that, there are 186 Olympic Provinces in the whole Universe, wherein the seven Governors do exercise their power: all which are elegantly set forth in Agronomy. But in this place it is to be explained, in what manner these Princes and Powers may be drawn into communication. Aratron appears in the first hour of Saturday, and very truely gives answers concerning his Provinces and Provincials. So likewise do the rest appear in order in their days and hours. Also every one of them rules 490 years. The beginning of their simple Anomaly, in the 60 year before the Nativity of Christ, was the beginning of the administration of Bethor; and it lasted until the year of our Lord Christ 430. To whom succeeded Phaleg, until the 920 year. Then began Och and continued until the year 1410. and thenceforth Hagith rules until the year 1900. [1]

---

[1] And at the time of the Theophania Publication of this book, 2011, we are in the first quarter of Ophiel's rule. Ed.

Aphor. 17.

Magically the Princes of the seven Governors are called simply, in that time, day, and hour wherein they rule visibly or invisibly, by their Names and Offices which God has given unto them; and by proposing their Character which they have given or confirmed. The Governor Aratron has in his power those things which he does naturally, that is, after the same manner and subject as those things which in Astronomy are ascribed to the power of Saturn. Those things which he does of his own free will, are:

1. That he can convert any thing into a stone in a moment, either animal or plant, retaining the same object to the fight.
2. He converts treasures into coals, and coals into treasure.
3. He gives familiars with a definite power.
4. He teachs Alchemy, Magick, and Physick.
5. He reconciles the subterranean spirits to men; makes hairy men.
6. He causes one to be invisible.
7. The barren he makes fruitful, and gives long life.

He has under him 49 Kings, 42 Princes, 35 Presidents, 28 Dukes, 21 Ministers, standing before him; 14 familiars, 7 messengers: he commands 36000 legions of spirits; the number of a legion is 490.

Bether governs those things which are ascribed to Jupiter: he soon comes being called. He that is dignified with his character, he raises to very great dignities to cast open treasures: he reconciles the spirits of the air, that they give true answers: they transport precious stones from place to place, and they make medicines to work miraculously in their effects: he gives also the familiars of the firmament, and prolongs life to 700 yeares if God will

His Character

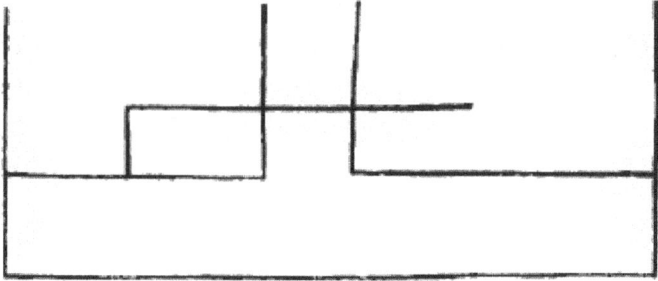

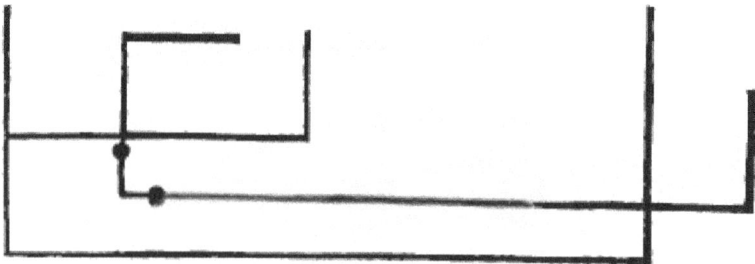

He has under him 42 Kings, 35 Princes, 28 Dukes, 21 Counsellors, 14 Ministers, 7 Messengers, 29000 legions of Spirits.

Phaleg rules those things which are attributed to Mars, the Prince of peace. He that has his character, he raises to great honours in warlike affairs.

His Character

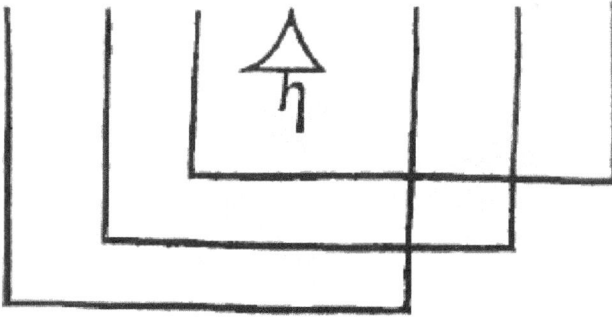

Och govems solar things; he gives 600 years, with perfect health; he bestows great wisdom, gives the most excellent Spirits, teachs perfect Medicines: he converts all things into most pure gold and precious stones: he gives gold, and a purse springing with gold. He that is dignified with his Character, he makes him to be worshipped as a Deity, by the Kings of the whole world.

His Character

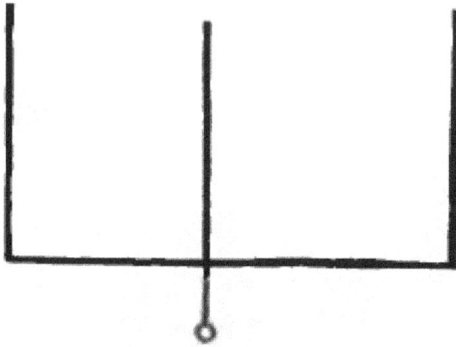

He has under him 36536 Legions: he administers all things alone: and all his spirits serve him by centuries.

Hagith governs Venereous things. He that, is dignified with his Character, he makes very fair, and to be adorned with all beauty. He converts copper into gold, in a moment, and gold into copper: he gives Spirits which do faithfully serve those to whom they are addicted.

His Character

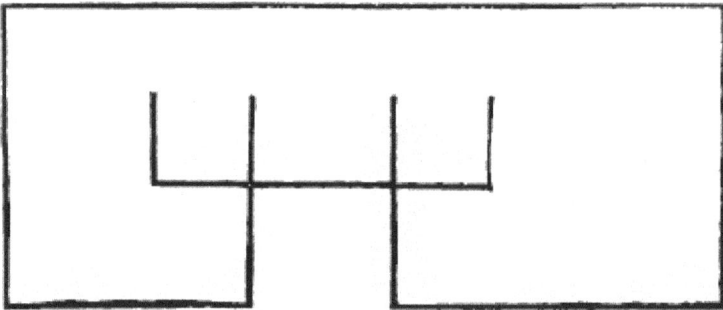

He has 4000 Legions of Spirits, and over every thousand he ordains Kings for their appointed seasons.

Ophiel is the governor of such things as are attributed to Mercury:

his Character is this.

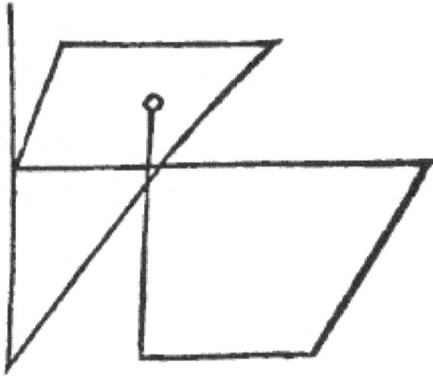

His Spirits are 100000 Legions: he easily gives Familiar Spirits: he teachs all Arts: and he that is dignified with his Character, he makes him to be able in a moment to convert Quicksilver into the Philosophers stone.

Phul has this Character.

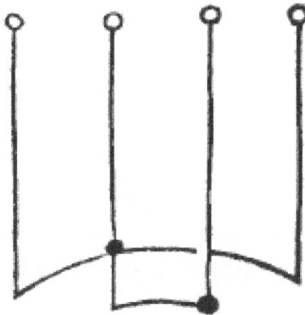

He changs all metals into silver, in word and deed governs Lunary things; heals the dropsie: he gives spirits of the water, who do serve men in a corporeal and visible form; and makes men to live 300 years.

1 . Every Governor acts with all his Spirits, either naturally, to wit, always after the same manner; or otherwise of their own free-will, if God hinder them not.

2. Every Governor is able to do all things which are done naturally in a long time, out of matter before prepared; and also to do them suddenly, out of matter not before prepared. As Och;, the Prince of Solar things, prepars gold in the mountains in a long time; in a less time, by the Chymical Art; and Magically, in a moment.

3 . The true and divine Magician may use all the creatures of God, and offices of the Governors of the world, at his own will, for that the Governors of the world are obedient unto them, and come when they are called, and do execute their commands: but God is the Author thereof: as Joshua caused the Sun to stand still in heaven. They send some of their Spirits to the mean Magicians, which do obey them only in some determinate business: but they hear not the false Magicians, but expose them to the deceits of the devils, and cast them into divers dangers, by the command of God; as the Prophet Jeremiah testifies, in his eighth Chapter, concerning the Jews.

4. In all the elements there are the seven Governors with their hosts, who do move with the equal motion of the firmament; and the inferiours do always depend upon the superiours, as it is taught in Philosophy.

5. A man that is a true Magician, is brought forth a Magician from his mothers womb: others, who do give themselves to this office, are unhappy. This is that which John the Baptist

speaks of: No man can do any thing of himself, except it be given him from above. Every Character given from a Spirit, for what cause soever, has his efficacy in this business, for which it is given, in the time prefixed: But it is to be used the same day and Planetary hour wherein it is given.

7. God lives, and your soul lives: keep your Covenant, and you have whatsoever the Spirit shall reveal unto you in God, because all things shall be done which the Spirit promises unto you.

Aphor. 18.

There are other names of the Olympic spirits delivered by others; but they only are effectual, which are delivered to any one, by the Spirit the revealer, visible or invisible: and they are delivered to every one as they are predestinated: therefore they are called Constellations; and they seldom have any efficacy above 40 years. Therefore it is most safe for the young practicers of Art, that they work by the offices of the Spirits alone, without their names; and if they are pre-ordained to attain the Art of Magick, the other parts of the Art will offer themselves unto them of their own accord. Pray therefore for a conntant faith, and God will bring to pass all things in due season.

Aphor. 19.

Olympus and the inhabitants thereof, do of their own accord offer themselves to men in the forms of Spirits; and are ready to perform their Offices for them, where they will or not: by how much the rather will they attend you, if they are desired? But there do appear also evil Spirits, and destroyers, which is called by the envy and malice of the devil; and because men do allure and draw them unto themselves with their sins, as a punishment due to sinners. Whomever therefore desires familiarly to have a conversation with Spirits, let him keep himself from all enormous sins, and diligently pray to the most High to be his keeper; and he shall break through all the snares and impediments of the devil: and let him apply himself to the service of God, and he will give him an increase in wisdom.

Aphor. 20.

All things are possible to them that believe them, and are willing to receive them; but to the incredulous and unwilling, all things are impossible: there is no greater hinderance then a wavering mind, levity, inconstancy, foolish babbling, drunkenness, lusts, and disobedience to the word of God. A Magician therefore ought to be a man that is godly, honest, constant in his words and deeds, having a firm faith towards God, prudent, and covetous of nothing but of wisdom about divine things.

Aphor. 21.

When you would call any of the Olympic Spirits, observe the rising of the Sun that day, and of what nature the Spirit is which you desire; and saying the prayer following, your desires shall be perfected.

Omnipotent and eternal God, who has ordained the whole creation for your praise and glory, and for the salvation of man, I beseech you that you would send your Spirit N. N. of the solar order, who shall inform and teach me those things which I shall ask of him; or, that he may bring me medicine against the dropsie, &C. Nevertheless not my will be done, but thine, through Jesus Christ your only begotten Son, our Lord. Amen.

But you shall not detain the Spirit above a full hour, unless he be familiarly addicted unto you.

Forasmuch at you came in peace, and quietly, and have answered unto my petitions; I give thanks unto God, in whose Name you came: and now you may depart in peace unto your orders; and return to me again when when called upon by your name, or by your order, or by your office, which is granted from the Creator, Amen.

Ecclesiast. Chap. 5. *Be not rash with your mouth, neither let your heart be hasty to utter any thing before God; for God is in Heaven, and you in earth: Therefore let your words be few; for a dream comes through the multitude of business.*

The fourth Septenary of Aphorisms.

The twenty-second Aphorism,

We call that a secret, which no man can attain unto by human industry without revelation; which Science lies obscured, hidden by God in the creature; which nevertheless he does permit to be revealed by Spirits, to a due use of the thing itself. And these secrets are either concerning things divine, natural or human. But you may examine a few, and the most select, which you will commend with many more.

Aphor. 23.

Make the beginning of the nature of the secret, either by a Spirit in the form of a person, or by venues separate, either in human Organs, or by what manner soever the same may be effected; and this being known, require of a Spirit which knowes that are, that he would briefly declare unto you whatsoever that secret is, and pray unto God, that he would inspire you with his grace, whereby you may bring the secret to the end you desire, for the praise and glory of God, and the profit of your neigbour.

Aphor. 24.

The greatest secrets are in number seven.

1. Thefirst is the curing of all diseases in the space of seven days, either by characters, or by natural things, or by the superior Spirits with the divine assistance.

2. The second is to be able to prolong life to whatsoever age we please: I say a corporal and natural life.

3. The third is to have the obedience of the creatures in in the elements which are in the forms of personal Spirits; spirits of also of Pigmies, Sagani, Nymphs, Dryads, and Spirits of the woods.

4. The fourth is, to be able to discourse with knowledge and understanding of all things visible and invisible, and to understand the power of every thing, and to what it belongs.

5. The fifth is, that a man be able to govern himself according to that end for which God has appointed him.

6. The sixth is, to know God, and Christ, and his holy Spirit: this is the perfection of the Microcosmus.

7. The seventh, to be regenerate, as Henochius theKing of the inferiour world. These seven secrets a man of an honest and constant mind may learn of the Spirits, without any offence unto God.

The mean Secrets are Likewise seven in number,

1. Thefirst is, the transmutation of Metals, which is vulgarly called Alchemy; which certainly is given to very few, and not but of special grace.

2. The second is, the curing of diseases with Metals, either by the magnetic virtues of precious stones, or by the use of the Philosophers stone, and the like.

3. The third is, to be able to perform Agronomical and Mathematical miracles, such as are Hydraulic engines, to administer business by the influence of Heaven, and things which are of the like sort.

4. The fourth is to perform the works of natural Magic, of what sort soever they be.

5. The fifth is, to know all Physical secrets.

6. The sixth is, to know the foundation of all Arts which are exercised with the hands and offices of the body.

7. The seventh is, to know the foundation of all Arts which are exercised by the angelical nature of man.

The lesser secrets are seven.

1 . The first is, to do a thing diligently, and to gather together much money.

2 . The second is to ascend from a mean state to dignities and honours, and to establish a newer family, which may be illustrious and do great things.

3. The third is to excel in military affairs, and happily to achieve to great things, and to be an head of the head of Kings and Princes.

4. To be a good House-keeper both in the Country and City.

5. The fifth is, to be an indubious and Fortunate Merchant.

6. To be a Philosopher, Mathematician, and Physician, according to Arislotle, Plato, Ptolomy, Euclides; Hippocrates and Galen.

7. To be a Divine according to the Bible and Schools, which all writers of divinity both old and new have taught.

Aphor. 25.

We have already declared what a secret is, the kinds and species thereof: it remains now to show how we may attain to know those things which we desire. The true and only way to all secrets, is to have recourse unto God the Author of all good; and as Christ teachs, In the first place seek you the kingdom of Cod and his righteousness, and all these things shall be added unto you.

2. Also see that your heart be not burdened with surfeiting, and drunkeness and the cares of this life.

3. Also commit your cares unto the Lord, and he will do it.

4. Also I the Lord your God do teach you, what things are profitable for you, and do guide you in the way wherein you walk.

5. And I will give you understanding, and will teach you in the way wherein you shall go, and I will guide you with my eye.

6. Also if you which are evil, know how to give good things to your children, how much more shall your Father which is in heaven give his holy Spirit to them that ask him?

7. If you will do the will of my Father which is in heaven, you are tritely my disciples, and we will come unto you, and make our abode with you. If you draw these seven places of Scripture from the letter unto the Spirit, or into action, you cannot err, but shall attain to the desired bound; you shall not err from the mark, and God himself by his holy Spirit

will teach you true and profitable things: he will give also his ministering Angels unto you, to be your companions, helpers, and teachers of all the secrets of the world, and he will command every creature to be obedient unto you, so that cheerfully rejoicing you may say with the Apostles, That the Spirits are obedient unto you; so that at length you shall be certain of the greatest thing of all, That your name is written in Heaven.

Aphor. 26.

There is another way which is more common, that secrets may be revealed unto you also, when you are unwitting thereof, either by God, or by Spirits which have secrets in their power; or by dreams, or by strong imaginations and impressions, or by the constellation of a nativity by celestial knowledge. After this manner are made heroic men, such as there are very many, and all learned men in the World, Plato, Arislrotle, Hippocrates, Galen, Euclides, Archimedes, Hermes Trismegistus the father of secrets, with Theophractus, Paracelcus; all which men had in themselves all the virtues of secrets. Hitherto also are referred, Homer, Hesiod, Orpheus, Pythagoras; but these had not such gifts of secrets as the former. To this are referred, the Nymphs, and sons of Melusina, and Gods of the Gentiles, Achilles, Æneas, Hercules; also Cyrus, Alexander the great, Julius Caesar, Lucullus, Sylla, Marius. It is a canon, that every one know his own Angel, and that he obey him according to the Word of God; and let him beware of the snares of the evil Angel, lest he be involved in the calamities of Brute and

Marcus Antonius. To this refer th ebook of Jovianus Pontanus of Fortune, and his Eutichus. The third way is, diligent and hard labor, without which no great thing can be obtained from the divine Deity worthy admiration, as it is said,

Tu nihil invita, dices faciesve Minerva.
Nothing can you do or say against Minerva's will.

We do detest all evil Magicians, who make themselves associates with the devils with their unlawful superstitions, and do obtain and effect some things which God permitts to be done, instead of the punishment of the devils. So also they do other evil acts, the devil being the authors the Scriptures testify of Judas. To these are referred all idolaters of old, and of our age, and abusers of Fortune, such as the heathens are full of. And to these do appertain all Charontick evocation of Spirits, as the work of Saul with the woman, and Lucanus prophecy of the deceased souldier, concerning the event of the Pharsalian war, and the like.

Aphor. 27.

Make a Circle with a center A, which is B.C.D.E. At the East let there be B. C. a square. At the North,C.D. At the West,D.E. And at the South,E.D. Divide the several quadrants into seven parts, that there may be in the whole 28 parts: and let them be again divided into four parts, that there may be 112 parts of the Circle: and so many are the true secrets to be revealed. And this Circle in this manner divided, is the seal of the secrets of the world, which they draw from the only center A, that is, from the invisible God, unto the whole creature. The Prince of the Oriental secrets is refident in the middle, and has three Nobles on either side, every one whereof has four under him, and the Prince himself has four appertaining unto him. And in this manner the other Princes and Nobles have their quadrants of secrets, with their four secrets. But the Oriental secret is the study of all wisdom; The West, of strength; The South, of tillage; The North, of more rigid life. So that the Eastern secrets are commended so be the best; the Meridian to be mean; and the East and North to be lesser. The use of this seal of secrets is, that thereby you may know whence the Spirits or Angels are produced, which may teach the secrets delivered unto them from God. But they have names taken from their offices and powers, according to the gift which God has severally distributed to every one of them. One has the power of the sword; another, of the pestilence; and another, of inflicting famine upon the people, as it is ordained by God. Some are destroyers of Cities, as those two were, who were sent to overthrow Sodom and Gomorrha; and the places adjacent, examples whereof the holy Scripture witnesses. Some are the watch-men over Kingdoms; others, the keepers of private persons; and from thence, anyone may easily form their names in his own language: so that he which will, may ask a physical Angel, mathematical, or philosophical, or an Angel or civil wisdom, or of supernatural or natural wisdom, or for any thing whatsoever; and let him ask seriously, with a great desire of his mind, and with faith and constancy; and without doubt, that which he asks he shall receive from the Father and God of all Spirits. This faith surmounts all seals, and brings them into subjection to the will of man. The Characteristical manner of calling Angles succeeds this faith, which depends only on divine revelation; But without the said faith preceding it, it is in obscurity. Nevertheless, if any one will use them for a memorial, and not otherwise, and as a thing simply created by God to this purpose, to which such a spiritual power or effence is bound; he may use them without any offence unto God. But let him beware, lest that he fall into idolatry, and the snares of the devil, who with his cunning sorceries, easily deceives the unwary. And he is not taken but only by the finger of God, and as appointed to the service of man; so that they unwillingly serve the godly; but not without temptations and tribulations, because the commandment has it, That he shall bruise the heel of Christ, the seed of the woman. We are therefore to exercise ourselves about spiritual things, with fear and trembling, and with great reverence towards God, and to be conversant in spiritual effences with gravity and justice. And he which meddles with such things, let him beware of all levity, pride, covetousness, vanity, envy and ungodliness, unless he will miserably perish.

Aphor. 28.

Because all good is from God, who is only good, those things which we would obtain of him, we ought to seek them by prayer in Spirit and Truth, and a simple heart. The conclusion of the secret of secrets is, That every one exercise himself in prayer, for those things which he desires, and he shall not suffer a repulse. Let not any one despise prayer; for by whom God is prayed unto, to him he both can and will give. Now let us acknowledge him the Author, from whom let us humbly seek for our desires. A merciful and good Father, loves the sons of desires, as Daniel; and sooner hears us,then we are able to overcome the hardness of our hearts to pray. But he will not that we give holy things to dogs, nor despise and condemn the gifts of his treasury. Therefore diligently and often read over and over the first Septenary of secrets, and guide and divest your life and all your thoughts according to those precepts; and all things shall yield to the desires of your mind in the Lord, to whom you trust.

The fifth Septenary of Aphorisms.

The twenty-ninth Aphorism,

As our study of Magick proceeds in order from general Rules premised, let us now come to a particular explication thereof. Spirits either are divine ministers of the word, and of the Church, and the members thereof; or else they are servient to the Creatures in corporal things, partly for the salvation of the soul and body, and partly for its destruction. And there is nothing done, whether good or evil, without a certain and determinate order and government. He that seeks after a good end, let him follow it; and he that desires an evil end, pursue that also, and that earnestly, from divine punishment, and turning away from the divine will. Therefore let every one compare his ends with the word of God, and as a touchstone that will judge between good and evil; and let him propose unto himself what is to be avoided, and what is to be sought after; and that which he constitutes and determines unto himself, let him follow diligently , not procrastinating or delaying, until he attain to his appointed bound.

Aphor. 30.

They which desire riches, glory of this world, Magiftracy, honours,digniiies,tyrannies, (and that magically) if they endeavour diligently after them, they shall obtain them, every one according to hisdefiiny, induflry, and magical Sciences, as the Hiftory of MeUfina witnefss, and the

Magitians thereof,who ordained,That none of the Italian
nation fhould for ever obtain the Rule or Kingdom of
Naples; and brought it to pafs, that he who reigned in his
age, to be thrown down from his feat r so great is the power
of the guardian or tutelar Angels of the Kingdoms of the
world.

Aphor. 31.

Call the Prince of the Kingdom, and lay a command upon
him, and command what you will, and it shall be done, if
that Prince be not again absolved from his obedience by a
succeeding Magician. Therefore the Kingdom of Naples may
be again restored to the Italians, if any Magician shall call
him who instituted this order, and compel him to recall his
deed; he may be compelled also, to restore the secret powers
taken from the treasury of Magick; A Book, a Gem, and
magical Horn, which being had, any one may easily, if he
will, make himself the Monarch of the world. But Judeus
chose rather to live among Gods, until the judgement,
before the transitory good of this world; and his heart is so
blind, that he understands nothing of the God of heaven
and earth, or thinks more, but enjoys the delights of things
immortal, to his own eternal destruction. And he may be
easier called up, then the Angel of Plotinus in the Temple of
Isis.

Aphor. 32.

In like manner also, the Romans were taught by the Sibyls books; and by that means made themselves the Lords of the world, as Histories witness. But the Lords of the Prince of a Kingdom do bestow, the lesser Magistracies. He therefore that desires to have a lesser office, or dignity, let him magically call a Noble of the Prince, and his desire shall be fulfilled.

Aphor. 33.

But he who covets contemptible dignities, as riches alone, let him call the Prince of riches, or one of his Lords, and he shall obtain his desire in that kind, whereby he would grow rich, either in earthly goods, or merchandise, or with the gifts of Princes, or by the study of Metals, or Chemistry: as he produces any president of growing rich by these means, he shall obtain his desire therein.

Aphor. 34.

All manner of evocation is of the same kind and form, and this way was familiar of old time to the Sibyls and chief Priests. This in our time, through ignorance and impiety, is totally lost; and that which remains, is depraved with infinite lies and superstitions.

Aphor. 35.

The human understanding is the only effecter of all wonderful works, so that it be joined to any Spirit; and being joined, she produces what she will. Therefore we are carefull to proceed in Magick, lest that Sirens and other monsters deceive us, which likewise do desire the society of the human soul. Let the Magician carefully hide himself always under the wings of the most High, lest he offer himself to be devoured of the roaring Lion; for they who desire earthly things, do very hardly escape the snares of the devil.

The thirty-sixth Aphorism,

Care is to be taken, that experiments be not mixed with experiments; but that every one be only simple and several: for God and Nature have ordained all things to a certain and appointed end: so that for examples sake, they who perform cures with the most simple herbs and roots, do cure the most happily of all. And in this manner, in Constellations, Words and Characters, Stones, and such like, do lie hid the greatest influences or virtues in deed, which are instead of a miracle. So also are words, which being pronounced, do forthwith cause creatures both visible and invisible to yield obedience, as well creatures of this our world, as of the watery, airy, subterranean, and Olympic, supercelestial and infernal, and also the divine. Therefore simplicity is chiefly to be studied, and the knowledge of such simples is to be sought for from God; otherwise by no other means or experience they can be found out.

Aphor. 37.

And let all lots have their place decently: Order, Reason and Means, are the three things which do easily render all learning as well of the visible as invisible creatures. This is the course of Order, That some creatures are creatures of the light; others, of darkness: these are subject to vanity, because they run headlong into darkness, and enthrall themselves in eternal punishments for their rebellion. Their Kingdom is partly very beautiful in transitory and corruptible things on the one part, because it cannot consist without some vertue and great gifts of God; and partly most filthy and horrid to be spoken of, because it abounds with all wickedness and sin, idolatry, contempt of God, blasphemies against the true God and his works, worshipping of devils, disobedience towards Magistrates, seditions, homicides, robberies, tyranny, adulteries, wicked lusts, rapes, thefts, lies, perjuries, pride, and a covetous desire of rule; in this mixture consists the kingdom of darkness: but the creatures of the light, are filled with eternal truth, and with the grace of God, and are Lords of the whole world, and do reign over the lords of darkness, as the members of Christ. Between these and the other, there is a continual war, until God shall put an end to their strife, by his last judgement.

Aphor. 38.

Therefore Magick is twofold in its first division; the one is ofGod, which he bestows on the creatures of light; the other also is of God,but it is the gift which he gives unto the creatures of darkness: and this is also two-fold: the one is to a good end, as when the Princes of darkness are compelled to do good unto the creatures, God enforcing them; the other is for an evil end, when God permitts such to punish evil persons, that magically they are deceived to destruction; or, also he commands such to be cast out into destruction. The second division of Magick is, that it brings to pass some works with visible instruments, through visible things; and it effects other works with invisible instruments by invisible things; and it acts other things, as well with mixed means, as increments and effects. The third division is, There are some things which are brought to pass by invocation of God alone: this is partly Prophetical, and Philosophical; and partly, as it were Theophractical. Other things there are, which by reason of the ignorance of the true God, are done with the Princes of Spirits, that his desires may be fulfilled; such is the work of the Mercurialists. The fourth division is, That some exercise their Magick with the good Angels instead of God, as it were descending down from the most high God: such was the Magick of Baalim. Another Magick is that which exercises their actions with the chief of the evil Spirits; such were they who wrought by the minor Gods of the heathens. The fifth division is, that some do act with Spirits openly, and face to face; which is given to few: others do work by dreams and other signs; which the ancients took from their auguries and sacrifices. The sixth division is, that some work by immortal creatures, others by mortal creatures, as Nymphs, Satyrs, and such-like inhabitants of other elements, Pigmies, &c. The seventh division is, that the Spirits do serve some of their own accord; without art; others they will scarce attend, being called by art. Among these species of Magick, that is the most excellent of all, which depends upon God alone. The second, they whom the Spirits do serve faithfully of their own accord. The third is, that which is the property of Christians, which depends on the power of Christ which he has, in heaven and earth.

Aphor. 39.

There is a seven-fold preparation to learn the Magick Art.

The first is, to meditate day and night how to attain to the true knowledge of God, both by his word revealed from the foundation of the world; as also by the seal of the creation, and of the creatures; and by the wonderful effects which the visible and invisible creatures of God do show forth. Secondly, it is requisite that a man descend down into himself, and chiefly study to know himself; what mortal pain he has in him, and what immortal; and what part is proper to himself, and what diverse. Thirdly, That he learn by the immortal part of himself, to worship, love and fear the eternal God, and to adore him in Spirit and Truth; and with his mortal part, to do those things which he knows to be acceptable to God, and profitable to his neighbours. These are the three first and chiefest precepts of Magick, wherewith let every one prepare himself that covers to obtain true Magick or divine wisdom, that he may be accounted worthy thereof, and one to whom the Angelical creatures willingly do service, not occultly only, but also manifestly, and as it were face to face. Fourthly, Whereas every man is to be vigilant to see to what kind life he shall be called from his mothers womb, that every one may know whether he be born to Magick, and to what species thereof, which every one may perceive easily that reads these things, and by experience may have success therein; for such things and such gifts are not given but only to the low and humble. In the fifth place we are to take care, that we understand when the Spirits are assisting us, in undertaking the greatest business; and he that understands this, it is manifest, that he shall be made a Magician of the ordination of God; that is, such a person who uses the ministery of the Spirits to bring excellent things to pass. Here, as for the most part, they sin, either through negligence, ignorance, or contempt, or by too much superstition; they offend also by ingratitude towards God, whereby many famous men have afterwards drawn upon themselves definition: they sin also by rashness and obstinacy; and also when they do not use their gifts for that honor of God which is required, and do prefer περιργα εργοις. Sixthly, The Magitian has need of faith and taciturnity, especially, that he disclofe no fsecret which the Spirit has forbid him, as he commanded Daniel to seal some things, that is, not to declare them in public; so as it was not lawful for Paul to speak openly of all things which he saw in a vision. No man will believe how much is contained in this one precept. Seventhly, In him that would be a Magician, there is required the greateft justice, that he undertake nothing that is ungodly, wicked or unjust, nor to let it once come in his mind; and so he shall be divinely defended from all evil.

Aphor. 40.

When the Magician determines with himself to do any incoporeal thing either with any exterior or interior sense, then let him govern himself according to these seven subsequent laws,to accomplish his Magical end. The first Law is this, That he know that such a Spirit is ordained unto him from God; and let him meditate that God is the beholder of all his thoughts and actions; therefore let him divest all the course of his life according to the rule prescribed in the word of God. Secondly, Always pray with David, *Take not your holy Spirit from me; and strengthen me with your free Spirit; and lead me not into temptation, but deliver me from evil: I beseech you, O heavenly Father, do not give power unto any lying Spirit, at you didst over Ahab that be perished, but keep me in your truth. Amen.* Thirdly, Let him accustom himself to try the Spirits, as the Scripture admonishs; for grapes cannot be gathered of thorns: let us try all things, and hold fast that which is good and laudable, that we may avoid every thing that is repugnant to the divine power. The fourth is, To be remote and clear from all manner of superstition; for this is superstition, to attribute divinity in this place to things, wherein there is nothing at all divine; or to choose or frame to our selves, to worship God with some kind of worship which he has not commanded: such are the Magical ceremonies of Satan,whereby he impudently offers himself to be worshipped as God. The fifth thing to be eschewed, is all worship of Idols, which binds any divine power to idols or other things of their own proper motion, where they are not placed by the Creator, or by the order of Nature: which things many false and wicked Magicians feign. Sixthly, All the deceitful imitations and affections of the devil are also to be avoided, whereby he imitates the power of the creation, and of the Creator, that he may so produce things with a word, that they may not be what they are, which belongs only to the Omnipotency of God, and is not communicable to the creature. Seventhly, Let us cleave fast to the gifts of

God, and of his holy Spirit, that we may know them, and diligently embrace them with our whole heart, and all our strength.

Aphor. 41.

We come now to the nine last Aphorisms of this whole Tome; where with we will, the divine mercy assisting us, conclude this whole Magical Isagoge. Therefore in the first place it is to be observed, what we understand by Magician in this work. Him then we count to be a Magician, to whom by the grace of God, the spiritual essences do serve to manifest the knowledge of the whole universe, and of the secrets of Nature contained therein, whether they are visible or invisible. This description of a Magician plainly appears, and is universal. An evil Magician is he, whom by the divine permission the evil Spirits do serve, to his temporal and eternal definition and perdition, to deceive men, and draw them away from God; such was Simon Magus, of whom mention is made in the Acts of the Apostles and in Clemens; whom Saint Peter commanded to be thrown down upon the earth, whenas he had commanded himself, as it were a God, to be railed up into the air by the unclean Spirits. Unto this order are also to be referred all those who are noted in the two Tables of the Law; and are set forth with their evil deeds. The subdivisions and species of both kinds of Magick, we will note in the Tomes following. In this place it shall suffice, that we distinguish the Sciences, which is good, and which is evil: Whereas man sought to obtain them both at first, to his own ruin and destruction, as Moses and Hermes do demonstrate.

47

Secondly, we are to know, That a Magician is a person predestinated to this work from his mothers womb; neither let him assume any such great things to himself, unless he be called divinely by grace hereunto, for some good end; to a bad end is, that the Scripture might be fufilled/, it must be that offences will come; but woe be to that man through whom they come. Therefore, as we have before oftentimes admonished, With fear and trembling we must live in this world. Notwithstanding I will not deny, but that some men may with study and diligence obtain some species of both kinds of Magick, if it may be admitted. But he shall never aspire to the highest kinds thereof; yet if he covet to assail them, he shall doubtless offend both in soul and body. Such are they, who by the operations of false Magicians, are sometimes carried to Mount Horeb or in some wilderness, or deserts; or they are maimed in some member, or are simply torn in pieces, or are deprived of their understanding; even as many such things happen by the use thereof, where men are forsaken by God, and delivered to the power of Satan.

The seventh Septenary of Aphorisms.

The fourty-third Aphorism,

The Lord lives, and the works of God do live in him by his appointment, whereby he wills them to be; for he will have them to use their liberty in obedience to his commands, or disobedience thereof. To the obedient, he has proposed their rewards; to the disobedient he has propounded their deserved punishment. Therefore these Spirits of their freewill, through their pride and contempt of the Son of God, have revolted from God their Creator and are reserved unto the day of wrath; and there is left in them a very great power in the creation; but notwithstanding it is limited, and they are confined to their bounds with the bridle of God. Therefore the Magician of God,which signifies a wise man of God, or one informed of God, is led forth by the hand of God unto all everlasting good, both mean things, and also the chiefest corporal things. Great is the power of Satan, by reason of the great sins of men. Therefore also the Magicians of Satan do perform great things, and greater then any man would believe: although they do subsist in their own limits, nevertheless they are above all human apprehension, as to the corporal and transitory things of this life; which many ancient Histories, and daily Examples do testify. Both kinds of Magic are different one from the other in their ends: the one leads to eternal good, and uses temporal things with thanksgiving; the other is a little sollicitous about eternal things; but wholly exercises himself about corporal things, that he may freely enjoy all his lusts and delights in contempt of God and his anger.

Aphor. 42.

The passage from the common life of man unto a Magical life, is no other but a sleep, from that life; and an awaking to this life; for those things which happen to ignorant and unwise men in their common life, the same things happen to the willing and knowing Magician. The Magician understands when the mind does meditate of himself; he deliberates, reasons, constitutes and determines what is to be done; he observes when his cogitations do proceed from a divine separate essence, and he proves of what order that divine separate essence is. But the man that is ignorant of Magick, is carried to and fro, as it were in war with his affections; he knows not when they issue out of his own mind, or are impressed by the assisting essence; and he knows not how to overthrow the counsels of his enemies by the word of God, or to keep himself from the snares and deceits of the tempter.

Aphor. 45.

The greatest precept of Magick is, to know what every man ought to receive for his life from the assisting Spirit, and what to refuse: which he may learn of the Psalmist, saying, *Wherewith shall a young man cleanse his way? in keeping your word, Oh Lord.* To keep the word of God, so that the evil one snatch it not out of the heart, is the chiefest precept of

50

wisdom. It is lawful to admit of, and exercise other suggestions which are not contrary to the glory of God, and charity towards our neighbours, not inquiring from what Spirit such suggestions proceed: But we ought to take heed, that we are not too much busied about unnecessary things, according to the admonition of Christ; *Martha, Martha, you are troubled about many things; but Mary has chosen the better part, which shall not be taken from her. Therefore let us always have regard unto the saying of Christ, Seek you first the Kingdom of God and his righteousness, and all these things shall be added unto you.* All other things, that is, all things which are due to the mortal Microcosm as food, raiment, and the necessary arts of this life.

Aphor. 46.

There is nothing so much becomes a man, as constancy in his words and deeds, and when the like rejoices in his like; there are none more happy than such, because the holy Angels are conversant about such, and possess the custody of them: on the contrary, men that are unconstant are lighter then nothing, and rotten leaves. We chose the 46 Aphorism from these. Even as every one governs himself, so he allures unto himself Spirits of his nature and condition; but one very truely advise, that no man should carry himself beyond his own calling, lest that he draw unto himself some malignant Spirit from the uttermost parts of the earth, by whom either he shall be infatuated and deceived, or brought to final destruction. This precept appears most plainly: for Midas, when he would convert all things into gold, drew up such a Spirit unto himself, which was able to perform this; and being deceived by him, he had been brought to death by famine, if his foolishness had not been corrected by the mercy of God. The same thing happened to a certain woman about Fanckford at Odera, in our times, who would scrape together and devour many of anything. Would that men would diligently weigh this precept, and not account the Histories of Midas, and the like, for fables; they would be much more diligent in moderating their thoughts and affections, neither would they be so perpetually vexed with the Spirits of the golden mountains of Utopia. Therefore we ought most diligently to observe, that such presumptions should be cast out of the mind, by the word, while they are new; neither let them have any habit in the idle mind, that is empty of the divine word.

Aphor. 47.

He that is faithfully conversant in his vocation, shall have also the Spirits constant companions of his desires, who will successively supply him in all things. But if he have any knowledge in Magick, they will not be unwilling to show him, and familiarly to converse with him, and to serve him in those several ministeries, unto which they are addicted; the good Spirits in good things, unto salvation; the evil Spirits in every evil thing, to destruction. Examples are not wanting in the Histories of the whole World; and do daily happen in the world. Theodosius before the victory of Arbogastus, is an example of the good; Brute before he was slain, was an example of the evil Spirits, when he was persecuted of the Spirit of Caesar, and exposed to punishment, that he slew himself, who had slain his own Father, and the Father of his Country.

Aphor. 48.

All Magick is a revelation of Spirits of that kind, of which sort the Magick is; so that the nine Muses are called, in Hesiod, the ninth Magick, as he manifestly testifys of himself in Theogony. In Homer, the genius of Ulysses in Psigiogagia. Hermes, the Spirits of the more sublime parts of the mind. God revealed himself to Moses in the bush. The three wise men who came to seek Christ ar Jerusalem, the Angel of the Lord was their leader. The Angels of the Lord directed Daniel. Therefore there is nothing whereof any one may glory; For it is not unto him that wills, nor unto him that ruins; but to whom God will have mercy, or of some other spiritual fate. From hence springs all Magick, and thither again it will revolve, whether it be good or evil. In this manner Tages the first teacher of the Magick of the Romans, gushed out of the earth. Diana of the Ephesians showed her worship, as if it had been sent from heaven. So also Apollo. And all the Religion of the Heathens is taken from the same Spirits; neither are the opinions of the Sadduces, human inventions.

The last aphorism of this tome:

Aphor. 49.

The conclusion therefore of this Isagoge is the same which we have above already spoken of, That even as there is one God, from whence is all good; and one sin, to wit, disobedience, against the will of the commanding God, From whence comes all evil; so that the *fear of God is the Beginning of all wisdom,* and the profit of all Magick; for obedience to the will of God, follows the fear of God; and after this, do follow the presence of God and of the holy Spirit, the ministry of the holy Angels, and all good things out of the inexhaustible creatures of God. But unprofitable and damnable Magick arises from this; where we lose the fear of God out of our hearts, and suffer sin to reign in us, there the Prince of this world, the God of this world begins, and sets up his kingdom in stead of holy things, in such as he finds profitable for his kingdom; there,even as the spider takes the fly which falls into his web, so Satan spreads abroad his nets and takes men with the snares of covetousness, until he sucks him, and draws him to eternal fire: these he cherishs and advances on high, that their fall may be the greater. Courteous Reader, apply your eyes and mind to the sacred and profane Histories, and to those things which you see daily to be done in the world; and you shall find all things full of Magick, according to a two-fold Science, good and evil, which that they may be the better discerned, we will put here, their division and subdivision, for the conclusion of these Isagoges; wherein every one may contemplate, what is to be followed, and which to be avoided, and how far it is to belabored for by every one,to a competent end of life and living.

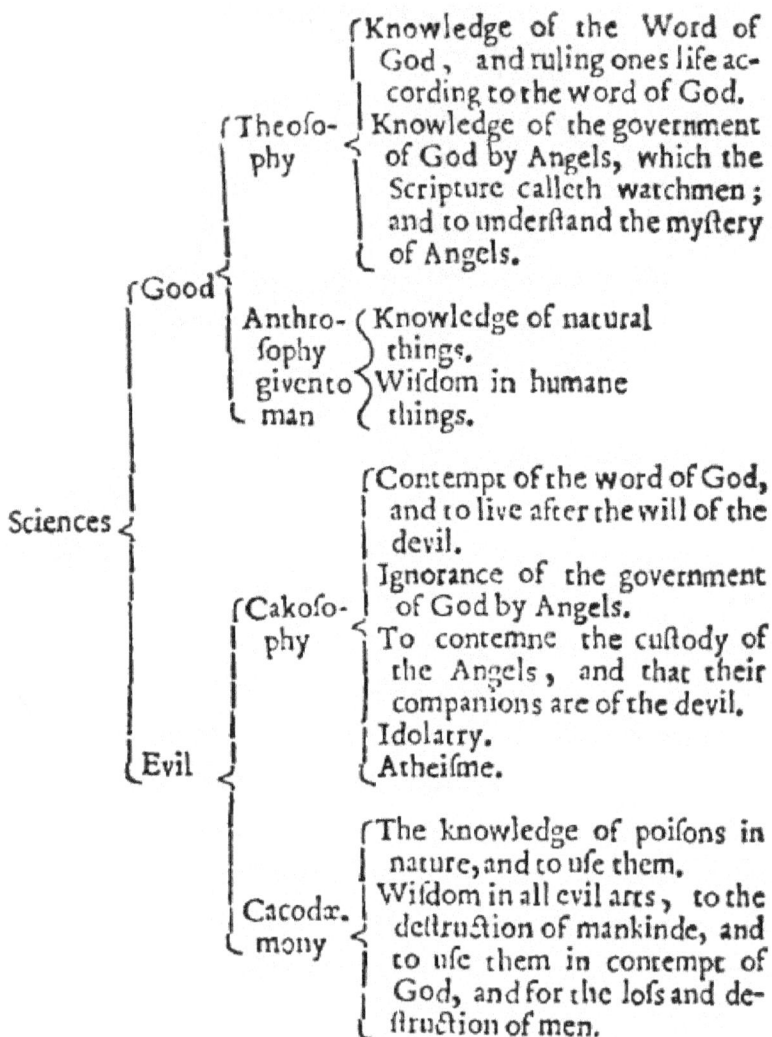

Sciences {

Good {

Theoso-phy {
Knowledge of the Word of God, and ruling ones life according to the word of God.

Knowledge of the government of God by Angels, which the Scripture calleth watchmen; and to understand the mystery of Angels.
}

Anthro-sophy given to man {
Knowledge of natural things.

Wisdom in humane things.
}
}

Evil {

Cakoso-phy {
Contempt of the word of God, and to live after the will of the devil.

Ignorance of the government of God by Angels.

To contemne the custody of the Angels, and that their companions are of the devil.

Idolatry.

Atheisme.
}

Cacodæ-mony {
The knowledge of poisons in nature, and to use them.

Wisdom in all evil arts, to the destruction of mankinde, and to use them in contempt of God, and for the loss and destruction of men.
}
}
}

FINIS.

www.ingramcontent.com/pod-product-compliance
Lightning Source LLC
Chambersburg PA
CBHW071751090426
42738CB00011B/2635